This Book Belongs

to

_____

Copyright © 2025 by Julie Bettendorf

All rights reserved.

No portion of this book may be reproduced in any form without written permission from the publisher or author, except as permitted by U.S. copyright law.

Hi, my name is Julie Bettendorf, and I am a traveler. During my travels, I have learned of many ghost stories, local lore, and strange happenings. Many of these phenomena are in this book. <u>Paranormal Journal: A Ghost Hunter's Companion</u> is meant to provide you with inspiration and space to document your experiences at home and on the road. All the best, and happy travels!

Clifford Griffin was an English bachelor who lived in Silver Plume, Colorado. He enjoyed playing the fiddle and drinking. Clifford led a tragic life. It seems his soon-to-be bride was strangled right before their wedding. Clifford became a recluse, sitting alone in his cabin, but serenading the citizens of Silver Plume with his fiddle at night. As the years went by, Clifford became more crazed, and his music became more frenzied. Then, on the night of June 10, 1887, Clifford shot himself and fell into a crude grave he had carved out previously. His ghost can still be heard playing the fiddle in the hills above Silver Plume.

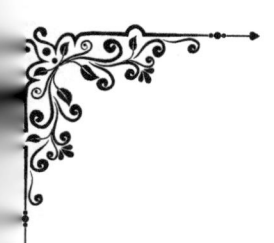

Date _____

Date _____

Date _____

Date ——————————

Date _____

Olga, Anne, and Josephine Johnson lost their lives on the night of January 2, 1890, when an avalanche knocked the Johnson home across the Yankee Fork, in Custer, Idaho. The parents, Nels and Maria Johnson both survived. The ghosts of the three Johnson girls are said to inhabit Custer. They've been seen walking hand-in-hand up the path to the remains of their old house.

Date _____

Date _____

Date _____

Date ———————————

Date _____

There is a building at La Purisima Mission in California that was once a jail. This building is said to be haunted by the ghost of a young vaquero who was murdered by another man. It seems the two were in love with the same woman and one of the men lured the other into the building, stabbed him to death, and buried him beneath a section of wall. His ghost is said to produce the icy feeling many visitors experience when they enter the building.

Date _____

Date _____

Date _____

Date _____

Date _____

The Pioneer Saloon in Goodsprings, Nevada, is said to be haunted by a cheating card player named Paul Coski. He was shot and killed while sitting at a poker table. You can see bullet holes in the ceiling which are thought to be from the shooting. Some have seen the ghosts of Carole Lombard and Clark Gable in the saloon. It was here in 1942 that Gable got the news Lombard had been killed in an airplane crash. There is a spot at the bar where Gable's cigarettes burned the wood where he was sitting, waiting for news.

Date _____

Date _____

Date _____

Date _____

Date ———————————

There have been tales of ghosts in Portland, Oregon's Underground. One such tale is that of crewmembers being shanghaied onto a ship named the Jennifer Jo. The men were viciously beaten and drugged before being loaded onto the ship and chained below deck. The ship left Portland with the shanghaied men, but the ship later sank in the Columbia River. The men below decks, still chained, drowned. Reports of being touched by wet hands, screaming, and moaning have been experienced in Portland's Underground. Some say it is the shanghaied men returned from the Jennifer Jo.

Date _____

Date _____

Date _____

Date _____

Date _____

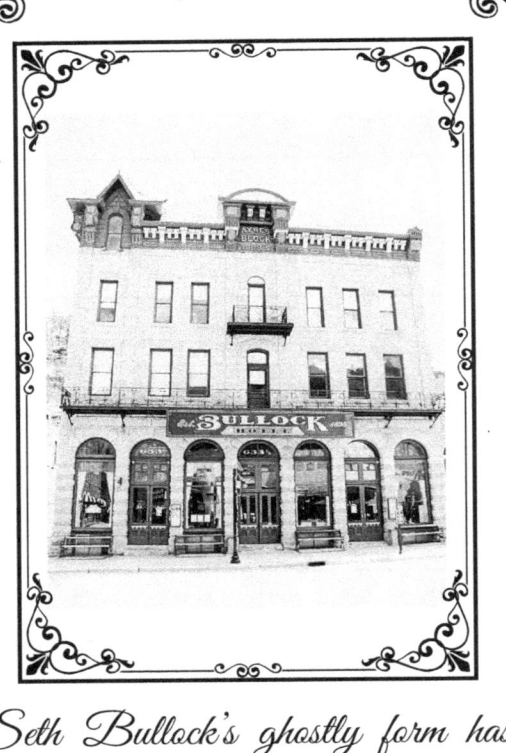

Marshall Seth Bullock's ghostly form has been sighted walking the halls of the Bullock Hotel in Deadwood, South Dakota. The most famous story is that of a young child who got locked out of his bedroom. He was helped back to his room by a kindly older man. The next day, the boy identified the man who helped him, from a picture on the wall. The picture was of Seth Bullock. Items in Seth's Cellar Restaurant have been seen moving on their own. No less than five people witnessed a glass come flying off a shelf and crashing to the floor. Still others have witnessed a "cowboy" roaming the halls and smoking a cigar.

Date _____

Date _____

Date ───────────────

Date _____

There is a tavern on the Boonslick Trail, in Missouri, which is haunted by the ghost of a young child. The ghost can be heard weeping, sobbing, and pulling blankets off of guests. A traveling minister came to the tavern, and the only room available was the haunted room. The minister believed God would protect him, so he rented the room. He heard the sobbing child and asked what was bothering the poor child. The child answered "I want a Christian burial. I was murdered and cannot rest." Workmen tore a hole in the wall, uncovering the remains of a child. The minister buried the child, and after that, the hauntings stopped. Soon afterwards, a workman confessed to accidentally striking and killing the poor child, and placing the child's body in the wall. He plastered over the wall, sealing in the remains.

Date _____

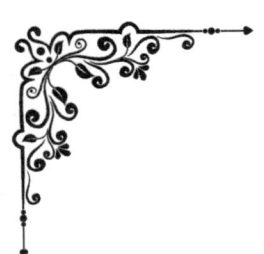

Date _____

Date _____

Date _____

Date ―――――――――――――

Chief Seattle's daughter, Kikisoblu, known also as Princess Angeline by early Seattle residents, lived at the foot of Pike Street. She sold baskets and did laundry to support herself. She died at age 85 on May 31, 1896. Her ghost has been seen on the lower levels of the Pike Place Market, close to where she used to live. She is a slow-moving figure, using a cane, and she wears a red kerchief on her head.

Date _____

Date _____

Date _____

Date _____

Date _____

The Whaley House, in San Diego's Old Town, was described by Life Magazine and others as "the number one most haunted house in America" because of the many ghosts and supernatural phenomena experienced there. Several hangings were conducted on the spot before the house was built on the site. Some of these unfortunates, including a man named Yankee Jim Robinson have been seen at Whaley House. Yankee Jim was hung for grand larceny back in 1852. The house is also said to have Thomas Whaley himself haunting the place, along with Violet Whaley, who committed suicide in the house in 1885.

Date _____

Date _____

Date _____

Date _____

Date _____

Libbie Custer and the officer's wives were gathered at the Custer house, in Fort Abraham Lincoln, North Dakota, when they received news of the massacre of all the soldiers, including their husbands, at the Battle of the Little Bighorn. Visitors and employees at the fort have seen a woman, dressed in black, standing at one of the upstairs windows. The bed in the upstairs bedroom will also occasionally show the imprint of a body weighing it down. paranormal investigators have also recorded a spirit voice saying "more of the men have been dying."

Date ―――――――――――――――――――――

Date ―――――――――――――

Date _____

Date _____

Date _____

Fort Laramie, Wyoming, is home to "The Lady in Green" who appears once every seven years. The story tells of the daughter of one of the founding fur traders, who had a cultured upbringing and was a highly skilled horsewoman. One day she went riding out alone, dressed in a beautiful, green riding habit. She was never seen again, alive anyway. The first documented sighting of the Lady in Green was in 1871, when she was seen by a young lieutenant from West Point, while he was out on horseback, hunting with some friends. This same lieutenant tried to follow her but could find no trace of her or her beautiful black horse.

Date _____

Date ───────────

Date _____

Date _____

Date _____

The Yaquina Head Lighthouse, near Newport, Oregon, has a noisy ghost. The lighthouse has both inner and outer walls. During construction in 1873, workers were filling in the space between the walls with rubble. A construction worker fell in between the walls. They couldn't get his body out, so the man was forever entombed in the lighthouse. Occasional hammering against the walls has been heard by visitors.

Date ――――――――――

Date _____

Date ───────────────────────

The Griffon, a small sailing ship, set sail on August 7, 1679, on her first voyage to Green Bay. There were 32 men on board. Once reaching Green Bay, a large cargo of furs was loaded. She left Green Bay on September 18, with a crew of 6. Bound for Niagara, the ship went missing. The light keeper of Manitoulin island on Lake Huron, reported finding five or six skeletons in a cave, before the turn of the century. One of the skeletons was very large, and it has been reported that the Danish captain was a large man. Old French coins, brass buttons, and two old gold watches were found near the skeletons. Over the centuries, various sightings of the "phantom ship" have been recorded.

Date _____

Date _____

Date _____

Date ───────────────

Date _____

A Spanish officer, Juan Espinoza, fell in love with a beautiful young woman. He went to the witches who lived in the oldest house in Santa Fe. Juan paid the witches many pieces of gold and received a love potion. The potion didn't bring the desired result, and the lady married another man. Juan brandished a sword and demanded the witches give him back the gold. One of the witches tripped him, he fell and lost his sword. The witch picked up the sword and cut his head off with it. The ghost of Juan Espinoza is said to wander Vargas Street in April when he was murdered, looking for his head.

Date _____

Date _____

Date _____

Date _____

The Hotel Meade, in Bannack, Montana, was built in 1875. It is home to the ghost of a 16-year-old girl named Dorothy Dunn. In 1915, she drowned in nearby Grasshopper Creek. Her apparition has been seen dressed in a long blue dress, on the second floor of the hotel. It was a favorite hang-out of Dorothy and her friends. Many visitors to the hotel sense a cold feeling when they climb the elegant, curved staircase to the second floor.

Date _____

Date _____

Date _____

Date _____

Date _____

In historic Harper's Ferry, West Virginia, there is a townhouse which housed Union soldiers during the Civil War. The soldiers captured a young Confederate drummer boy and enslaved him. The boy was bullied constantly. He begged the men to let him go, so he could return to his mother. The men made a show of tossing him around and made as if to throw him out the window. They missed catching the boy, and he hit the street and died. People report hearing sounds of a boy crying and begging to go home to his mother.

Date _____

Date _____

Date _____

Date ──────────────

Date _____

The Mizpah Hotel in Tonopah, Nevada, has a ghost named the "Lady in Red." She is said to have been murdered there on the 5th floor. The Lady in Red was a prostitute who conducted her business with Mizpah patrons in the 1920s. A wealthy man is said to have killed her in a room on the fifth floor in a fit of rage after learning he was only one of her many customers. Legend has it that the ghost of the lady roams the hotel to this day. Another version of the tale says her husband caught the woman cheating on him at the hotel after he had missed a train. He beat her to death in a room, now often requested by guests who believe in the paranormal.

Date _____

Date _____

Date _____

Date _____

Date _____

Louisville, Kentucky, is the site of a large and beautiful area known as Iroquois Park. Land for the park was purchased in 1889. There is a legend about a couple building a homestead on the land in the early 1800s. The husband traveled to Louisville one night, leaving his wife at home alone. While he was gone, Indians attacked the homestead, killing the woman by cutting off her head. The apparition of the "Headless Lady of Iroquois Park" has been seen on several occasions.

Date _____

_____
_____
_____
_____
_____
_____
_____
_____
_____
_____
_____
_____
_____
_____
_____
_____
_____
_____
_____

Date _____

Date ————————————

Date _____

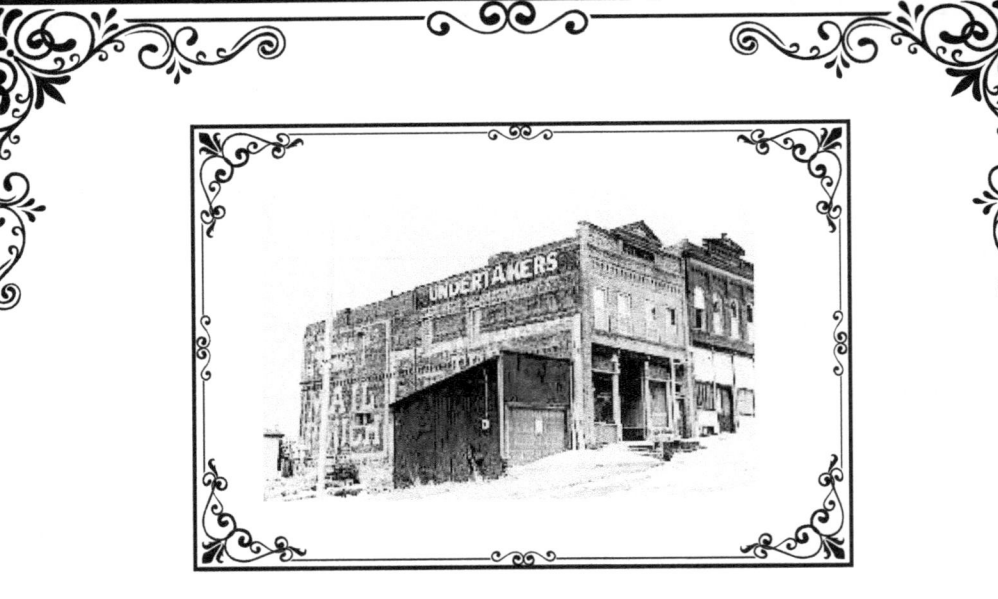

Thomas Dunn had a mortuary business on the first floor of the Dunn Building in Victor, Colorado. Dunn and an assistant were preparing a miner's mangled body, who was the victim of a cave-in. During preparations, the man began twitching, and then screaming. Dunn gave the poor man a dose of morphine and continued his preparations, assuming that the man would eventually die, which he did. Today there are reports of exploding light bulbs, slamming doors, and cold spots. Is it the poor unfortunate miner, or Thomas Dunn haunting the place? No one knows, but the word "Undertakers" still remain painted on the side of the building in tribute to Thomas Dunn and the poor miner.

Date _____

Date _____

Date ───────────────────────

Date _____

Date _____

The Moonshine Gulch Saloon in Rochford, South Dakota, is reportedly haunted by the ghost of the former owner. It is believed that the owner is buried underneath the building. In fact, the current owners found a tombstone believed to be hers. The tombstone now lies underneath part of the building. Paranormal happenings include objects dropping for no apparent reason, lights not working, and the feeling of someone brushing by visitors. Ghosts of miners have also been seen and noises of mining have been heard coming from the woods.

Date _____

Date _____

Date ―――――――――――――――

Date ───────────────

Date _____

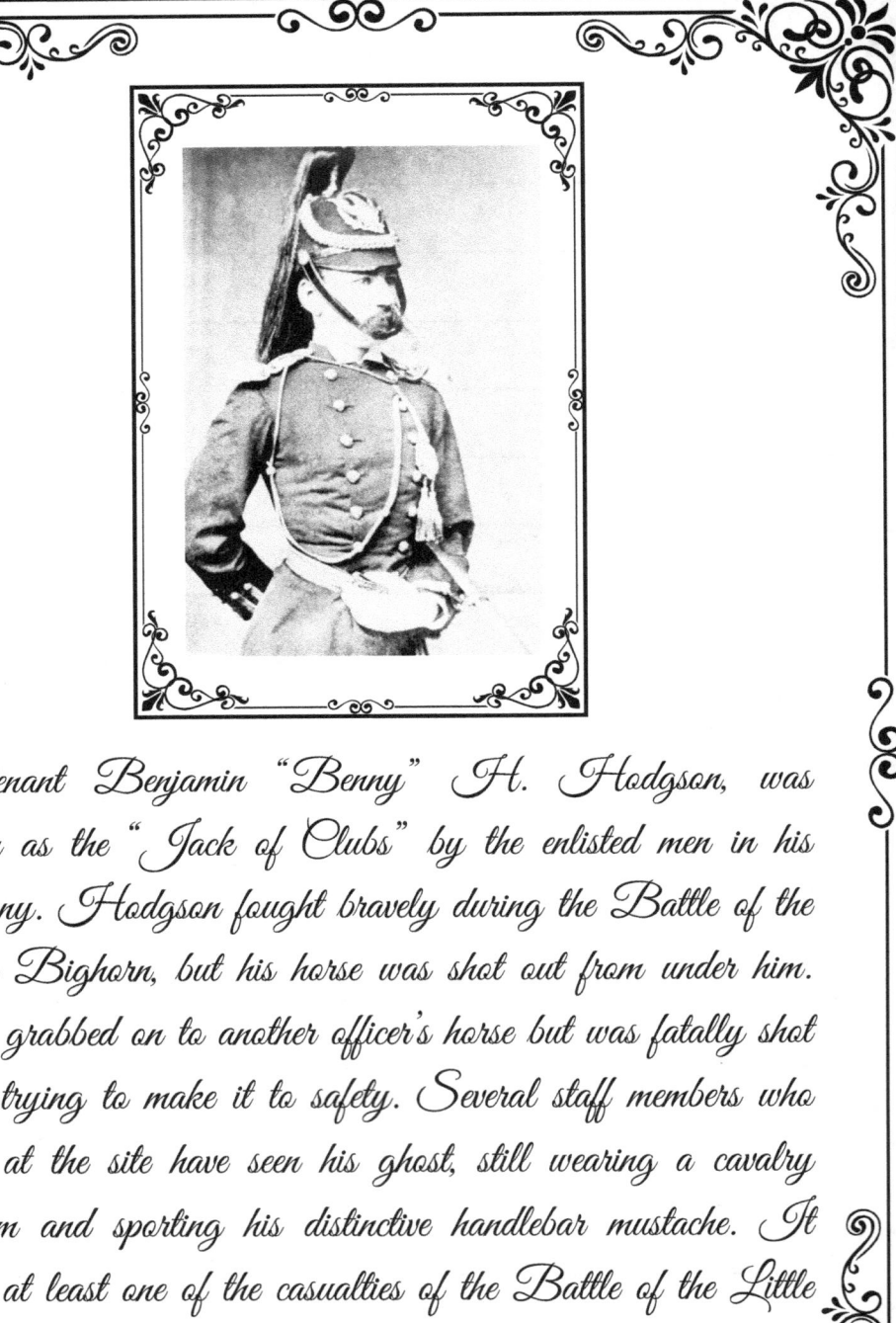

Lieutenant Benjamin "Benny" H. Hodgson, was known as the "Jack of Clubs" by the enlisted men in his company. Hodgson fought bravely during the Battle of the Little Bighorn, but his horse was shot out from under him. He grabbed on to another officer's horse but was fatally shot while trying to make it to safety. Several staff members who work at the site have seen his ghost, still wearing a cavalry uniform and sporting his distinctive handlebar mustache. It seems at least one of the casualties of the Battle of the Little Bighorn has never left.

Date _____

Date ───────────────

Date _____

Date _____

Date _____

Railroad engineer, Michael Ryan, suffered a head injury, which left him unable to work. By 1900 he was a penniless hermit. He often walked by the side of the road carrying a railroad lantern. By 1905, Ryan was living an isolated life in a shack, pelting intruders with rocks. In 1923, deep inside the Widow Maker Tunnel, through Ute Pass near Colorado Springs, human remains were found, alongside a crushed railroad lantern. Officials determined that the bones were Michael Ryan's and he was buried where he lay, inside the tunnel. Today, there are reports of flashes of light being seen at night, believed to be signals from long-dead railroad engineer Michael Ryan.

Date _____

Date _____

Date _____

Date _____

Fort Sisseton, South Dakota, was built over the top of an Indian burial ground. In fact, when the flagpole was raised in 1864, the remains of an Indian grave were found. A soldier is said to haunt the barracks, with the sound of his boots echoing on the floor. The sound his feet make is said to come from a pair of Jefferson Brogan boots with wooden soles held in place by brass nails. These boots were worn by soldiers in the infantry in the 1800s.

Date _____

Date _____

Date _____

The Delta Saloon, in Virginia City, Nevada, has a faro table, known as the "Suicide Table." "Black Jake" who owned the faro table, lost $70,000 in one night and promptly killed himself. In 1890, the new owner of the table lost $86,000 and also killed himself. The ghosts of these men and others are said to haunt the Delta Saloon.

Date _____

Date _____

Fort Hays, Kansas, has at least one ghost haunting the premises. A cholera epidemic hit Fort Hays and the surrounding area. Elizabeth Polly, who was wife to the fort doctor, helped to tend to the sick. Elizabeth soon became sick with cholera and requested to be buried on top of an area of the fort known as Sentinel Hill. The top of the hill was too rocky to dig a deep grave, so Elizabeth was buried on the side of the hill instead. Sightings of the ghost of Elizabeth began in 1897 and continue to the present. She is known as the "Blue Light Lady."

Date ___

Date _____

Date _____

Date _____

The Stones River Battlefield, in Tennessee, is inhabited by the ghosts of several soldiers. Apparitions have been fired upon by Civil War reenactors, only to have the apparition disappear. The most famous ghost is that of Lieutenant Colonel Julius Garesche. Garesche was chief of staff to General Rosecrans, who led the Union Army. While inspecting the Union lines on December 31, 1862, Garesche was shot and decapitated by the bullet. His headless corpse continued to ride the horse for twenty yards before falling. Garesche's ghost has come to be known as "The Headless Horseman of Stones River Battlefield."

Date _____

Date _____

Date _____

Date _____

Date

No one is sure when burials began in the Post Cemetery, of Fort Mackinac, Michigan, because there are both British and American soldiers from the War of 1812 buried there. There are 108 burials in the cemetery, only 39 of which are identified. There are several children also buried in the cemetery. The apparition of a woman has been seen, sitting in a corner, perhaps mourning her dead children. The ghost is believed to be the mother of Josiah and Isabel Cowles, who were buried in the cemetery in 1884, and 1888.

Date _____

Date _____

The many ghosts of Garnet, Montana, are more active in winter. The only access to Garnet in deep snow is by snowmobile, and people do rent out some of the cabins in winter. There is also a winter caretaker. Many spectral orbs and full-bodied apparitions have been seen which disappear before the eyes of startled cabin renters. Honky-tonk piano music, the tinkling of glasses, and spectral voices have been heard by winter caretakers.

Date _____

Date _____

Date _____

Date _____

The City Hotel, now a part of Columbia State Historic Park, in California, was built in 1856. It didn't start out haunted. An antique bed was brought over from the Midwest in the 1870s by a gentleman trying to make his fortune. He eventually sent for his wife, but she died on her way to California. The bed was passed among many antique dealers, but eventually was brought back to the City Hotel. Guests of the hotel have reported mournful sobbing, rose scented perfume, cold spots, and door rattling when they sleep in the bed. It is believed that a woman died in childbirth in room #1 that housed the bed.

Date _____

Date _____

Date _____

Date _____

Richard King, a realtor in Bonanza, Idaho, died leaving a grieving widow, Lizzie. She was supposed to marry Richard's friend, Charles Franklin, but she had other ideas. Instead, she married Robert Hawthorne, the new man in town. Lizzie and her new husband were later found dead, and the friend, Charles, had left town. He was eventually found dead, with her picture in a locket in his hand. The ghosts of Lizzie and Robert are said to inhabit the woods near Bonanza.

Date _____

Date _____

Date _____

Date _____

Date _____

The Goldfield Hotel is said to be haunted by a pair of ghosts, George Wingfield, who was part owner of the hotel and one of Nevada's wealthiest men at the time, and Elizabeth, a young prostitute, who was in love with Wingfield. Elizabeth became pregnant and Wingfield forced her to remain in seclusion in the hotel. She was chained to a radiator in room 109. She gave birth, and she died in the hotel, either by starvation or murder by George Wingfield. He then threw the newborn down a mineshaft under the hotel. Visitors have stated they smell Wingfield's cigar smoke and sense his malevolent presence. They also sense the sad presence of Elizabeth haunting room 109

Date _____

Date ───────────────

Date _____

Date _____

The ghost of Raymond Snowden may be haunting the execution chamber of the Old Idaho Penitentiary in Boise. Raymond Snowden was executed in 1957, but the execution didn't go smoothly. When Snowden dropped, his neck didn't break. Instead, he hung there for several desperate minutes before choking to death. Visitors to the execution chamber have reported hearing struggling sounds. One visitor even claimed to see Snowden's apparition hanging in the space.

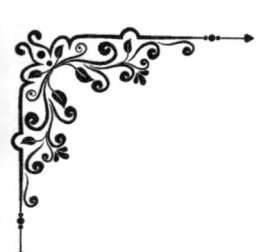

Date _____

Date ─────────────

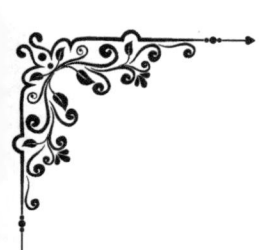

Date _____

Date _____

Date _____

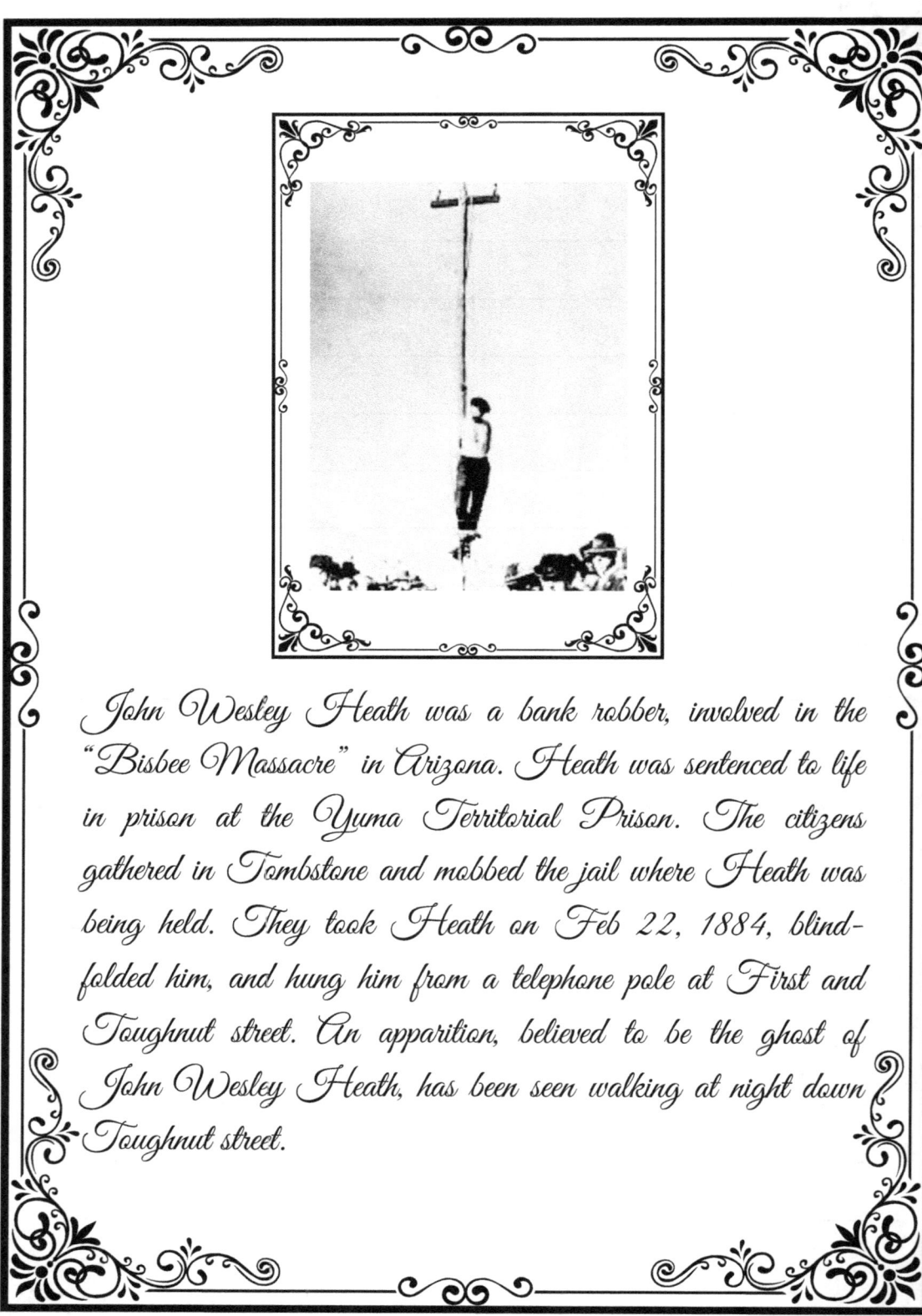

John Wesley Heath was a bank robber, involved in the "Bisbee Massacre" in Arizona. Heath was sentenced to life in prison at the Yuma Territorial Prison. The citizens gathered in Tombstone and mobbed the jail where Heath was being held. They took Heath on Feb 22, 1884, blindfolded him, and hung him from a telephone pole at First and Toughnut street. An apparition, believed to be the ghost of John Wesley Heath, has been seen walking at night down Toughnut street.

Final Thoughts

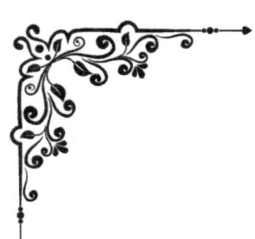

Sources:

Baumler, Ellen. *Montana Chillers: 13 True Tales of Ghosts and Hauntings*. Farcountry Incorporated, 2015.

Bottjer, Linda J. *Gold Rush Ghosts of Placerville, Coloma, and Georgetown*. Haunted America, a Division of The History Press, 2014.

Davis, Jefferson and Janine, *A Haunted Tour Guide to the Pacific Northwest*, Norsemen Ventures, 2010.

Dwyer, Jeff. *Ghost Hunter's Guide to California's Gold Rush Country*. Pelican Pub., 2009.

Glass, Dean. *The History & Mystery of the Whaley House*. Our Heritage Press, 2016.

Kitmacher, Ira Wesley, *Haunted Graveyard of the Pacific*, History Press, 2021.

Mayo, Matthew P. *Haunted Old West: Phantom Cowboys, Spir-it-Filled Saloons, Mystical Mine Camps, and Spectral Indians*. Globe Pequot Press, 2012.

Munn, Debra D. *Wyoming Ghost Stories: Eerie True Tales*. Riverbend, 2008.

Kitmacher, Ira Wesley, Haunted Graveyard of the Pacific, History Press, 2021.

Mayo, Matthew P. Haunted Old West: Phantom Cowboys, Spirit-Filled Saloons, Mystical Mine Camps, and Spectral Indians. Globe Pequot Press, 2012.

Munn, Debra D. Wyoming Ghost Stories: Eerie True Tales. Riverbend, 2008.

Oberding, Janice. Haunted Nevada: Ghosts and Strange Phenomena of the Silver State. Stackpole Books, 2013.

Oberding, Janice. Haunted Virginia City. Haunted America, a Division of the History Press, 2015.

Quackenbush, Jannette, West Virginia Ghost Stories, Legends, and Haunts, 21 Crows Publishing, 2017.

Senate, Richard. Ghosts of the California Missions. Shoreline Press, 2011.

Smith, B. Ghost Stories of the Rocky Mountains. Lone Pine Pub., 1999.

Stansfield, Charles A. Haunted Washington: Ghosts and Strange Phenomena of the Evergreen State. Stackpole Books, 2011.

Waters, Stephanie. Colorado Legends & Lore. The History Press, 2014.

Weeks, Andy. Haunted Idaho: Ghosts and Strange Phenomena of the Gem State. Stackpole Books, 2013.

Weeks, Andy. Haunted Oregon: Ghosts and Strange Phenomena of the Beaver State. Stackpole Books, 2014.

Wommack, Linda. Haunted Cripple Creek and Teller County. The History Press, 2018.

www.ingramcontent.com/pod-product-compliance
Lightning Source LLC
Chambersburg PA
CBHW080452100526
44581CB00004B/112